MONTHLY BILL

PLANNER & ORGNIZER

If found, please return to:
Name:
Address:
Telephone Number:
Email:

Special Notes

Special Notes

BILL PLANNER & ORGANIZER

Financial Goals ______________________________ Month ______________

Number	Goal
1	
2	
3	
4	
5	
6	
7	
8	
9	
10	
11	
12	
13	
14	
15	
16	
17	
18	
19	

BILL PLANNER & ORGANIZER

Payable to	Amount Due	Due On	Paid (yes/No)	Notes

TOTAL PAYABLES	$	Total Income	$
NET BALANCE (OVER/SHORT)	$		

BILL PLANNER & ORGANIZER

Financial Goals ______________________________ Month ______________

Number	Goal
1	
2	
3	
4	
5	
6	
7	
8	
9	
10	
11	
12	
13	
14	
15	
16	
17	
18	
19	

BILL PLANNER & ORGANIZER

Payable to	Amount Due	Due On	Paid (yes/No)	Notes

TOTAL PAYABLES	$	Total Income	$
NET BALANCE (OVER/SHORT)	$		

BILL PLANNER & ORGANIZER

Financial Goals ____ Month ____________________

Number	Goal
1	
2	
3	
4	
5	
6	
7	
8	
9	
10	
11	
12	
13	
14	
15	
16	
17	
18	
19	

BILL PLANNER & ORGANIZER

Payable to	Amount Due	Due On	Paid (yes/No)	Notes

TOTAL PAYABLES	$	Total Income	$
NET BALANCE (OVER/SHORT)	$		

BILL PLANNER & ORGANIZER

Financial Goals ______________________ Month ______________

Number	Goal
1	
2	
3	
4	
5	
6	
7	
8	
9	
10	
11	
12	
13	
14	
15	
16	
17	
18	
19	

BILL PLANNER & ORGANIZER

Payable to	Amount Due	Due On	Paid (yes/No)	Notes
TOTAL PAYABLES	$	Total Income		$
NET BALANCE (OVER/SHORT)	$			

BILL PLANNER & ORGANIZER

Financial Goals ______________________________ Month ______________

Number	Goal
1	
2	
3	
4	
5	
6	
7	
8	
9	
10	
11	
12	
13	
14	
15	
16	
17	
18	
19	

BILL PLANNER & ORGANIZER

Payable to	Amount Due	Due On	Paid (yes/No)	Notes

TOTAL PAYABLES	$	*Total Income*	$
NET BALANCE (OVER/SHORT)	$		

BILL PLANNER & ORGANIZER

Financial Goals ______________________________ Month ______________

Number	Goal
1	
2	
3	
4	
5	
6	
7	
8	
9	
10	
11	
12	
13	
14	
15	
16	
17	
18	
19	

BILL PLANNER & ORGANIZER

Payable to	Amount Due	Due On	Paid (yes/No)	Notes

TOTAL PAYABLES	$	*Total Income*	$
NET BALANCE (OVER/SHORT)	$		

BILL PLANNER & ORGANIZER

Financial Goals ____________________ Month ____________

Number	Goal
1	
2	
3	
4	
5	
6	
7	
8	
9	
10	
11	
12	
13	
14	
15	
16	
17	
18	
19	

BILL PLANNER & ORGANIZER

Payable to	Amount Due	Due On	Paid (yes/No)	Notes

TOTAL PAYABLES	$	Total Income	$
NET BALANCE (OVER/SHORT)	$		

BILL PLANNER & ORGANIZER

Financial Goals ______________________________ Month ______________

Number	Goal
1	
2	
3	
4	
5	
6	
7	
8	
9	
10	
11	
12	
13	
14	
15	
16	
17	
18	
19	

BILL PLANNER & ORGANIZER

Payable to	Amount Due	Due On	Paid (yes/No)	Notes
TOTAL PAYABLES	$	Total Income		$
NET BALANCE (OVER/SHORT)	$			

BILL PLANNER & ORGANIZER

Financial Goals ______________________________ Month ______________

Number	Goal
1	
2	
3	
4	
5	
6	
7	
8	
9	
10	
11	
12	
13	
14	
15	
16	
17	
18	
19	

BILL PLANNER & ORGANIZER

Payable to	Amount Due	Due On	Paid (yes/No)	Notes

TOTAL PAYABLES	$	Total Income	$
NET BALANCE (OVER/SHORT)	$		

BILL PLANNER & ORGANIZER

Financial Goals ______________________________ Month ______________

Number	Goal
1	
2	
3	
4	
5	
6	
7	
8	
9	
10	
11	
12	
13	
14	
15	
16	
17	
18	
19	

BILL PLANNER & ORGANIZER

Payable to	Amount Due	Due On	Paid (yes/No)	Notes
TOTAL PAYABLES	$	Total Income	$	
NET BALANCE (OVER/SHORT)	$			

BILL PLANNER & ORGANIZER

Financial Goals ______________________________ Month ____________

Number	Goal
1	
2	
3	
4	
5	
6	
7	
8	
9	
10	
11	
12	
13	
14	
15	
16	
17	
18	
19	

BILL PLANNER & ORGANIZER

Payable to	Amount Due	Due On	Paid (yes/No)	Notes
TOTAL PAYABLES	$	Total Income		$
NET BALANCE (OVER/SHORT)	$			

BILL PLANNER & ORGANIZER

Financial Goals ______________________________ Month ______________

Number	Goal
1	
2	
3	
4	
5	
6	
7	
8	
9	
10	
11	
12	
13	
14	
15	
16	
17	
18	
19	

BILL PLANNER & ORGANIZER

Payable to	Amount Due	Due On	Paid (yes/No)	Notes

TOTAL PAYABLES	$	Total Income	$
NET BALANCE (OVER/SHORT)	$		

BILL PLANNER & ORGANIZER

Financial Goals ______________________________ Month ______________

Number	Goal
1	
2	
3	
4	
5	
6	
7	
8	
9	
10	
11	
12	
13	
14	
15	
16	
17	
18	
19	

BILL PLANNER & ORGANIZER

Payable to	Amount Due	Due On	Paid (yes/No)	Notes
TOTAL PAYABLES	$	Total Income		$
NET BALANCE (OVER/SHORT)	$			

BILL PLANNER & ORGANIZER

Financial Goals ______________________________ Month ______________

Number	Goal
1	
2	
3	
4	
5	
6	
7	
8	
9	
10	
11	
12	
13	
14	
15	
16	
17	
18	
19	

BILL PLANNER & ORGANIZER

Payable to	Amount Due	Due On	Paid (yes/No)	Notes
TOTAL PAYABLES	$	Total Income		$
NET BALANCE (OVER/SHORT)	$			

BILL PLANNER & ORGANIZER

Financial Goals ______________________________ Month ______________

Number	Goal
1	
2	
3	
4	
5	
6	
7	
8	
9	
10	
11	
12	
13	
14	
15	
16	
17	
18	
19	

BILL PLANNER & ORGANIZER

Payable to	Amount Due	Due On	Paid (yes/No)	Notes
TOTAL PAYABLES	$	Total Income		$
NET BALANCE (OVER/SHORT)	$			

BILL PLANNER & ORGANIZER

Financial Goals ______________________________ *Month* ______________

Number	*Goal*
1	
2	
3	
4	
5	
6	
7	
8	
9	
10	
11	
12	
13	
14	
15	
16	
17	
18	
19	

BILL PLANNER & ORGANIZER

Payable to	Amount Due	Due On	Paid (yes/No)	Notes
TOTAL PAYABLES	$	Total Income		$
NET BALANCE (OVER/SHORT)	$			

BILL PLANNER & ORGANIZER

Financial Goals ______________________________ Month ______________

Number	Goal
1	
2	
3	
4	
5	
6	
7	
8	
9	
10	
11	
12	
13	
14	
15	
16	
17	
18	
19	

BILL PLANNER & ORGANIZER

Payable to	Amount Due	Due On	Paid (yes/No)	Notes

TOTAL PAYABLES	$	Total Income	$
NET BALANCE (OVER/SHORT)	$		

BILL PLANNER & ORGANIZER

Financial Goals ____________________ Month ____________

Number	Goal
1	
2	
3	
4	
5	
6	
7	
8	
9	
10	
11	
12	
13	
14	
15	
16	
17	
18	
19	

BILL PLANNER & ORGANIZER

Payable to	Amount Due	Due On	Paid (yes/No)	Notes

TOTAL PAYABLES	$	Total Income	$
NET BALANCE (OVER/SHORT)	$		

BILL PLANNER & ORGANIZER

Financial Goals ______________________________ Month ______________

Number	Goal
1	
2	
3	
4	
5	
6	
7	
8	
9	
10	
11	
12	
13	
14	
15	
16	
17	
18	
19	

BILL PLANNER & ORGANIZER

Payable to	Amount Due	Due On	Paid (yes/No)	Notes

TOTAL PAYABLES	$	Total Income	$
NET BALANCE (OVER/SHORT)	$		

BILL PLANNER & ORGANIZER

Financial Goals ______________________________ *Month* ____________

Number	Goal
1	
2	
3	
4	
5	
6	
7	
8	
9	
10	
11	
12	
13	
14	
15	
16	
17	
18	
19	

BILL PLANNER & ORGANIZER

Payable to	Amount Due	Due On	Paid (yes/No)	Notes
TOTAL PAYABLES	$	Total Income		$
NET BALANCE (OVER/SHORT)	$			

BILL PLANNER & ORGANIZER

Financial Goals ______________________________ Month ______________

Number	Goal
1	
2	
3	
4	
5	
6	
7	
8	
9	
10	
11	
12	
13	
14	
15	
16	
17	
18	
19	

BILL PLANNER & ORGANIZER

Payable to	Amount Due	Due On	Paid (yes/No)	Notes
TOTAL PAYABLES	$	Total Income		$
NET BALANCE (OVER/SHORT)	$			

BILL PLANNER & ORGANIZER

Financial Goals ______________________________ Month ______________

Number	Goal
1	
2	
3	
4	
5	
6	
7	
8	
9	
10	
11	
12	
13	
14	
15	
16	
17	
18	
19	

BILL PLANNER & ORGANIZER

Payable to	Amount Due	Due On	Paid (yes/No)	Notes
TOTAL PAYABLES	$	*Total Income*		$
NET BALANCE (OVER/SHORT)	$			

BILL PLANNER & ORGANIZER

Financial Goals ______________________________ Month ______________

Number	Goal
1	
2	
3	
4	
5	
6	
7	
8	
9	
10	
11	
12	
13	
14	
15	
16	
17	
18	
19	

BILL PLANNER & ORGANIZER

Payable to	Amount Due	Due On	Paid (yes/No)	Notes
TOTAL PAYABLES	$	Total Income		$
NET BALANCE (OVER/SHORT)	$			

BILL PLANNER & ORGANIZER

Financial Goals ______________________________ Month ______________

Number	Goal
1	
2	
3	
4	
5	
6	
7	
8	
9	
10	
11	
12	
13	
14	
15	
16	
17	
18	
19	

BILL PLANNER & ORGANIZER

Payable to	Amount Due	Due On	Paid (yes/No)	Notes
TOTAL PAYABLES	$	Total Income		$
NET BALANCE (OVER/SHORT)	$			

BILL PLANNER & ORGANIZER

Financial Goals ________________________________ Month ____________

Number	Goal
1	
2	
3	
4	
5	
6	
7	
8	
9	
10	
11	
12	
13	
14	
15	
16	
17	
18	
19	

BILL PLANNER & ORGANIZER

Payable to	Amount Due	Due On	Paid (yes/No)	Notes

TOTAL PAYABLES	$	Total Income	$
NET BALANCE (OVER/SHORT)	$		

BILL PLANNER & ORGANIZER

Financial Goals ______________________________ Month ______________

Number	Goal
1	
2	
3	
4	
5	
6	
7	
8	
9	
10	
11	
12	
13	
14	
15	
16	
17	
18	
19	

BILL PLANNER & ORGANIZER

Payable to	Amount Due	Due On	Paid (yes/No)	Notes

TOTAL PAYABLES	$	Total Income	$
NET BALANCE (OVER/SHORT)	$		

BILL PLANNER & ORGANIZER

Financial Goals ______________________________ Month ______________

Number	Goal
1	
2	
3	
4	
5	
6	
7	
8	
9	
10	
11	
12	
13	
14	
15	
16	
17	
18	
19	

BILL PLANNER & ORGANIZER

Payable to	Amount Due	Due On	Paid (yes/No)	Notes

TOTAL PAYABLES	$	Total Income	$
NET BALANCE (OVER/SHORT)	$		

BILL PLANNER & ORGANIZER

Financial Goals ________________________________ Month ______________

Number	Goal
1	
2	
3	
4	
5	
6	
7	
8	
9	
10	
11	
12	
13	
14	
15	
16	
17	
18	
19	

BILL PLANNER & ORGANIZER

Payable to	Amount Due	Due On	Paid (yes/No)	Notes

TOTAL PAYABLES	$	Total Income	$
NET BALANCE (OVER/SHORT)	$		

BILL PLANNER & ORGANIZER

Financial Goals ______________________________ Month ______________

Number	Goal
1	
2	
3	
4	
5	
6	
7	
8	
9	
10	
11	
12	
13	
14	
15	
16	
17	
18	
19	

BILL PLANNER & ORGANIZER

Payable to	Amount Due	Due On	Paid (yes/No)	Notes

TOTAL PAYABLES	$	Total Income	$
NET BALANCE (OVER/SHORT)	$		

BILL PLANNER & ORGANIZER

Financial Goals ______________________________ Month ______________

Number	Goal
1	
2	
3	
4	
5	
6	
7	
8	
9	
10	
11	
12	
13	
14	
15	
16	
17	
18	
19	

BILL PLANNER & ORGANIZER

Payable to	Amount Due	Due On	Paid (yes/No)	Notes
TOTAL PAYABLES	$	Total Income		$
NET BALANCE (OVER/SHORT)	$			

BILL PLANNER & ORGANIZER

Financial Goals ______________________________ Month ______________

Number	Goal
1	
2	
3	
4	
5	
6	
7	
8	
9	
10	
11	
12	
13	
14	
15	
16	
17	
18	
19	

BILL PLANNER & ORGANIZER

Payable to	Amount Due	Due On	Paid (yes/No)	Notes
TOTAL PAYABLES	$	Total Income		$
NET BALANCE (OVER/SHORT)	$			

BILL PLANNER & ORGANIZER

Financial Goals ______________________________ Month ______________

Number	Goal
1	
2	
3	
4	
5	
6	
7	
8	
9	
10	
11	
12	
13	
14	
15	
16	
17	
18	
19	

BILL PLANNER & ORGANIZER

Payable to	Amount Due	Due On	Paid (yes/No)	Notes
TOTAL PAYABLES	$	Total Income		$
NET BALANCE (OVER/SHORT)	$			

BILL PLANNER & ORGANIZER

Financial Goals ______________________________ Month ______________

Number	Goal
1	
2	
3	
4	
5	
6	
7	
8	
9	
10	
11	
12	
13	
14	
15	
16	
17	
18	
19	

BILL PLANNER & ORGANIZER

Payable to	Amount Due	Due On	Paid (yes/No)	Notes

TOTAL PAYABLES	$	Total Income	$
NET BALANCE (OVER/SHORT)	$		

BILL PLANNER & ORGANIZER

Financial Goals ______________________________ Month ______________

Number	Goal
1	
2	
3	
4	
5	
6	
7	
8	
9	
10	
11	
12	
13	
14	
15	
16	
17	
18	
19	

BILL PLANNER & ORGANIZER

Payable to	Amount Due	Due On	Paid (yes/No)	Notes
TOTAL PAYABLES	$	Total Income		$
NET BALANCE (OVER/SHORT)	$			

BILL PLANNER & ORGANIZER

Financial Goals ______________________________ Month ______________

Number	Goal
1	
2	
3	
4	
5	
6	
7	
8	
9	
10	
11	
12	
13	
14	
15	
16	
17	
18	
19	

BILL PLANNER & ORGANIZER

Payable to	Amount Due	Due On	Paid (yes/No)	Notes
TOTAL PAYABLES	$	Total Income	$	
NET BALANCE (OVER/SHORT)	$			

BILL PLANNER & ORGANIZER

Financial Goals ______________________________ Month ______________

Number	Goal
1	
2	
3	
4	
5	
6	
7	
8	
9	
10	
11	
12	
13	
14	
15	
16	
17	
18	
19	

BILL PLANNER & ORGANIZER

Payable to	Amount Due	Due On	Paid (yes/No)	Notes
TOTAL PAYABLES	$	Total Income	$	
NET BALANCE (OVER/SHORT)	$			

BILL PLANNER & ORGANIZER

Financial Goals ______________________________ Month ______________

Number	Goal
1	
2	
3	
4	
5	
6	
7	
8	
9	
10	
11	
12	
13	
14	
15	
16	
17	
18	
19	

BILL PLANNER & ORGANIZER

Payable to	Amount Due	Due On	Paid (yes/No)	Notes
TOTAL PAYABLES	$	Total Income	$	
NET BALANCE (OVER/SHORT)	$			

BILL PLANNER & ORGANIZER

Financial Goals ______________________________ Month ______________

Number	Goal
1	
2	
3	
4	
5	
6	
7	
8	
9	
10	
11	
12	
13	
14	
15	
16	
17	
18	
19	

BILL PLANNER & ORGANIZER

Payable to	Amount Due	Due On	Paid (yes/No)	Notes
TOTAL PAYABLES	$	Total Income		$
NET BALANCE (OVER/SHORT)	$			

BILL PLANNER & ORGANIZER

Financial Goals ________________________________ Month ______________

Number	Goal
1	
2	
3	
4	
5	
6	
7	
8	
9	
10	
11	
12	
13	
14	
15	
16	
17	
18	
19	

BILL PLANNER & ORGANIZER

Payable to	Amount Due	Due On	Paid (yes/No)	Notes
TOTAL PAYABLES	$	Total Income	$	
NET BALANCE (OVER/SHORT)	$			

BILL PLANNER & ORGANIZER

Financial Goals ________________________________ Month ______________

Number	Goal
1	
2	
3	
4	
5	
6	
7	
8	
9	
10	
11	
12	
13	
14	
15	
16	
17	
18	
19	

BILL PLANNER & ORGANIZER

Payable to	Amount Due	Due On	Paid (yes/No)	Notes
TOTAL PAYABLES	$	Total Income	$	
NET BALANCE (OVER/SHORT)	$			

BILL PLANNER & ORGANIZER

Financial Goals ______________________________ Month ______________

Number	Goal
1	
2	
3	
4	
5	
6	
7	
8	
9	
10	
11	
12	
13	
14	
15	
16	
17	
18	
19	

BILL PLANNER & ORGANIZER

Payable to	Amount Due	Due On	Paid (yes/No)	Notes

TOTAL PAYABLES	$	Total Income	$
NET BALANCE (OVER/SHORT)	$		

BILL PLANNER & ORGANIZER

Financial Goals ______________________________ Month ______________

Number	Goal
1	
2	
3	
4	
5	
6	
7	
8	
9	
10	
11	
12	
13	
14	
15	
16	
17	
18	
19	

BILL PLANNER & ORGANIZER

Payable to	Amount Due	Due On	Paid (yes/No)	Notes

TOTAL PAYABLES	$	Total Income	$
NET BALANCE (OVER/SHORT)	$		

BILL PLANNER & ORGANIZER

Financial Goals ______________________ Month ______________

Number	Goal
1	
2	
3	
4	
5	
6	
7	
8	
9	
10	
11	
12	
13	
14	
15	
16	
17	
18	
19	

BILL PLANNER & ORGANIZER

Payable to	Amount Due	Due On	Paid (yes/No)	Notes

TOTAL PAYABLES	$	Total Income	$
NET BALANCE (OVER/SHORT)	$		

BILL PLANNER & ORGANIZER

Financial Goals ______________________________ Month ______________

Number	Goal
1	
2	
3	
4	
5	
6	
7	
8	
9	
10	
11	
12	
13	
14	
15	
16	
17	
18	
19	

BILL PLANNER & ORGANIZER

Payable to	Amount Due	Due On	Paid (yes/No)	Notes
TOTAL PAYABLES	$	Total Income		$
NET BALANCE (OVER/SHORT)	$			

BILL PLANNER & ORGANIZER

Financial Goals ______________________________ *Month* ______________

Number	Goal
1	
2	
3	
4	
5	
6	
7	
8	
9	
10	
11	
12	
13	
14	
15	
16	
17	
18	
19	

BILL PLANNER & ORGANIZER

Payable to	Amount Due	Due On	Paid (yes/No)	Notes
TOTAL PAYABLES	$	Total Income		$
NET BALANCE (OVER/SHORT)	$			

BILL PLANNER & ORGANIZER

Financial Goals ______________________________ *Month* ______________

Number	Goal
1	
2	
3	
4	
5	
6	
7	
8	
9	
10	
11	
12	
13	
14	
15	
16	
17	
18	
19	

BILL PLANNER & ORGANIZER

Payable to	Amount Due	Due On	Paid (yes/No)	Notes
TOTAL PAYABLES	$	Total Income		$
NET BALANCE (OVER/SHORT)	$			

BILL PLANNER & ORGANIZER

Financial Goals ____ Month ____________________

Number	Goal
1	
2	
3	
4	
5	
6	
7	
8	
9	
10	
11	
12	
13	
14	
15	
16	
17	
18	
19	

BILL PLANNER & ORGANIZER

Payable to	Amount Due	Due On	Paid (yes/No)	Notes
TOTAL PAYABLES	$	Total Income	$	
NET BALANCE (OVER/SHORT)	$			

BILL PLANNER & ORGANIZER

Financial Goals ______________________________ Month ______________

Number	Goal
1	
2	
3	
4	
5	
6	
7	
8	
9	
10	
11	
12	
13	
14	
15	
16	
17	
18	
19	

BILL PLANNER & ORGANIZER

Payable to	Amount Due	Due On	Paid (yes/No)	Notes

TOTAL PAYABLES	$	Total Income	$
NET BALANCE (OVER/SHORT)	$		

BILL PLANNER & ORGANIZER

Financial Goals ______________________________ *Month* ______________

Number	Goal
1	
2	
3	
4	
5	
6	
7	
8	
9	
10	
11	
12	
13	
14	
15	
16	
17	
18	
19	

BILL PLANNER & ORGANIZER

Payable to	Amount Due	Due On	Paid (yes/No)	Notes
TOTAL PAYABLES	$	Total Income		$
NET BALANCE (OVER/SHORT)	$			

BILL PLANNER & ORGANIZER

Financial Goals ______________________________ Month ______________

Number	Goal
1	
2	
3	
4	
5	
6	
7	
8	
9	
10	
11	
12	
13	
14	
15	
16	
17	
18	
19	

BILL PLANNER & ORGANIZER

Payable to	Amount Due	Due On	Paid (yes/No)	Notes

TOTAL PAYABLES	$	Total Income	$
NET BALANCE (OVER/SHORT)	$		

BILL PLANNER & ORGANIZER

Financial Goals ______________________________ Month ______________

Number	Goal
1	
2	
3	
4	
5	
6	
7	
8	
9	
10	
11	
12	
13	
14	
15	
16	
17	
18	
19	

BILL PLANNER & ORGANIZER

Payable to	Amount Due	Due On	Paid (yes/No)	Notes

TOTAL PAYABLES	$	Total Income	$
NET BALANCE (OVER/SHORT)	$		

BILL PLANNER & ORGANIZER

Financial Goals ______________________________ Month ______________

Number	Goal
1	
2	
3	
4	
5	
6	
7	
8	
9	
10	
11	
12	
13	
14	
15	
16	
17	
18	
19	

BILL PLANNER & ORGANIZER

Payable to	Amount Due	Due On	Paid (yes/No)	Notes
TOTAL PAYABLES	$	Total Income	$	
NET BALANCE (OVER/SHORT)	$			

BILL PLANNER & ORGANIZER

Financial Goals ______________________________ Month ______________

Number	Goal
1	
2	
3	
4	
5	
6	
7	
8	
9	
10	
11	
12	
13	
14	
15	
16	
17	
18	
19	

BILL PLANNER & ORGANIZER

Payable to	Amount Due	Due On	Paid (yes/No)	Notes
TOTAL PAYABLES	$	Total Income		$
NET BALANCE (OVER/SHORT)	$			

BILL PLANNER & ORGANIZER

Financial Goals ______________________________ Month ______________

Number	Goal
1	
2	
3	
4	
5	
6	
7	
8	
9	
10	
11	
12	
13	
14	
15	
16	
17	
18	
19	

BILL PLANNER & ORGANIZER

Payable to	Amount Due	Due On	Paid (yes/No)	Notes
TOTAL PAYABLES	$	Total Income	$	
NET BALANCE (OVER/SHORT)	$			

BILL PLANNER & ORGANIZER

Financial Goals ______________________ Month ______________

Number	Goal
1	
2	
3	
4	
5	
6	
7	
8	
9	
10	
11	
12	
13	
14	
15	
16	
17	
18	
19	

BILL PLANNER & ORGANIZER

Payable to	Amount Due	Due On	Paid (yes/No)	Notes
TOTAL PAYABLES	$	Total Income		$
NET BALANCE (OVER/SHORT)	$			

BILL PLANNER & ORGANIZER

Financial Goals ________________________________ *Month* ______________

Number	Goal
1	
2	
3	
4	
5	
6	
7	
8	
9	
10	
11	
12	
13	
14	
15	
16	
17	
18	
19	

BILL PLANNER & ORGANIZER

Payable to	Amount Due	Due On	Paid (yes/No)	Notes
TOTAL PAYABLES	$	Total Income		$
NET BALANCE (OVER/SHORT)	$			

BILL PLANNER & ORGANIZER

Financial Goals ______________________________ Month ______________

Number	Goal
1	
2	
3	
4	
5	
6	
7	
8	
9	
10	
11	
12	
13	
14	
15	
16	
17	
18	
19	

BILL PLANNER & ORGANIZER

Payable to	Amount Due	Due On	Paid (yes/No)	Notes
TOTAL PAYABLES	$	Total Income		$
NET BALANCE (OVER/SHORT)	$			

BILL PLANNER & ORGANIZER

Financial Goals ______________________________ Month ______________

Number	Goal
1	
2	
3	
4	
5	
6	
7	
8	
9	
10	
11	
12	
13	
14	
15	
16	
17	
18	
19	

BILL PLANNER & ORGANIZER

Payable to	Amount Due	Due On	Paid (yes/No)	Notes

TOTAL PAYABLES	$	Total Income	$
NET BALANCE (OVER/SHORT)	$		

BILL PLANNER & ORGANIZER

Financial Goals ____________________ Month ____________

Number	Goal
1	
2	
3	
4	
5	
6	
7	
8	
9	
10	
11	
12	
13	
14	
15	
16	
17	
18	
19	

BILL PLANNER & ORGANIZER

Payable to	Amount Due	Due On	Paid (yes/No)	Notes

TOTAL PAYABLES	$	Total Income	$
NET BALANCE (OVER/SHORT)	$		

BILL PLANNER & ORGANIZER

Financial Goals ______________________________ Month ______________

Number	Goal
1	
2	
3	
4	
5	
6	
7	
8	
9	
10	
11	
12	
13	
14	
15	
16	
17	
18	
19	

BILL PLANNER & ORGANIZER

Payable to	Amount Due	Due On	Paid (yes/No)	Notes

TOTAL PAYABLES	$	Total Income	$
NET BALANCE (OVER/SHORT)	$		

BILL PLANNER & ORGANIZER

Financial Goals ______________________________ Month ______________

Number	Goal
1	
2	
3	
4	
5	
6	
7	
8	
9	
10	
11	
12	
13	
14	
15	
16	
17	
18	
19	

BILL PLANNER & ORGANIZER

Payable to	Amount Due	Due On	Paid (yes/No)	Notes

TOTAL PAYABLES	$	Total Income	$
NET BALANCE (OVER/SHORT)	$		

BILL PLANNER & ORGANIZER

Financial Goals ______________________________ Month ______________

Number	Goal
1	
2	
3	
4	
5	
6	
7	
8	
9	
10	
11	
12	
13	
14	
15	
16	
17	
18	
19	

BILL PLANNER & ORGANIZER

Payable to	Amount Due	Due On	Paid (yes/No)	Notes

TOTAL PAYABLES	$	Total Income	$
NET BALANCE (OVER/SHORT)	$		

CPSIA information can be obtained
at www.ICGtesting.com
Printed in the USA
LVOW09s1404081117
R12838800001B/R128388PG555190LVX1B/1/P

9 781542 618885